B⌾⌾T CAMP
for
MARRIAGES

Christy & Hope,

Thank you both again so much for your Hospitality & Friendship. It was so good to spend time with you all. Praying Gods Richest Blessings over you and your Family.

Mark 10:8

Darrin & Lashawn Aoon

BOOT CAMP *for* MARRIAGES

BY DARRIN and LASHAWN ADEN

XULON PRESS

Xulon Press
2301 Lucien Way #415
Maitland, FL 32751
407.339.4217
www.xulonpress.com

© 2020 by Darrin and LaShawn Aden

All rights reserved solely by the author. The author guarantees all contents are original and do not infringe upon the legal rights of any other person or work. No part of this book may be reproduced in any form without the permission of the author. The views expressed in this book are not necessarily those of the publisher.

Unless otherwise indicated, Scripture quotations taken from the English Standard Version (ESV). Copyright © 2001 by Crossway, a publishing ministry of Good News Publishers. Used by permission. All rights reserved.

Scripture quotations taken from the King James Version (KJV) – *public domain.*

Scripture quotations taken from the New King James Version (NKJV). Copyright © 1982 by Thomas Nelson, Inc. Used by permission. All rights reserved.

Scripture quotations taken from the Holy Bible, New Living Translation (NLT). Copyright ©1996, 2004, 2007 by Tyndale House Foundation. Used by permission of Tyndale House Publishers, Inc.

Printed in the United States of America.

ISBN-13: 978-1-6305-0590-5

Table of Contents

Introduction................................ix

1. Delayed Enlistment – Dating 1
2. Basic Training/Boot Camp –The Engagement ..11
3. Technical Training – Pre-Marital Counseling/ Coaching................................17
4. Commitment in Marriage 25
5. Communication in Marriage................35
6. Gender Roles in Marriage..................43
7. Conflict in Marriage 51
8. Financial Faithfulness in Marriage 63
9. Raising Godly Children 73
10. Graduation 81

Introduction

According to the article, "Younger Generations Are Doing It Differently," published by the World Economic Forum in 2018, divorce rates in the United States are dropping. On the surface, this statistic might sound like great news unless it is your family that's experiencing divorce. It is unfortunate but we all probably know someone whose family has been traumatized by the emotional scars of a divorce. In our opinion, divorce is not something anyone should subscribe to lightly without spiritual and/or professional counseling. Far too often, we see couples that would rather "throw in the towel" than work through a season of marriage counseling.

God created man and woman to be as one in marriage, and what He has joined together, let no one split apart. (Mark 10:8-9) Although we don't advocate divorce, we aren't naïve to think there aren't special circumstances and situations that could warrant or justify it. This is a strong reason why marriage counseling becomes so important. I believe King Solomon said it best, "Where no counsel is, the people fall: but in the multitude of counselors there is safety." (Prov. 11:14)

This year, my wife and I will celebrate over thirty-one years of marriage, to which we give God all the honor and glory. As we thought about the God-given assignment of writing this book, we soon realized how significant a part our military careers played in our marriage. It is our desire through this book that God will reveal to you winning strategies and principles for your marriage. Just as basic military training prepares each service member for their military careers, we pray this manual will help prepare you and your spouse for your life-long marriage together.

1.

Delayed Enlistment – Dating

One of the first programs essential to the success of any military recruit is the Delayed Enlistment program. During this program, the military recruiter is responsible for educating the trainee on future expectations, acceptable character and conduct, rules and regulations, physical requirements, and many other facets of military life. This can only be accomplished by spending time together and building a shared mutual trust in one another.

In a similar fashion, we see this exact same scenario play out in dating. As a couple spends time together, they discover qualities they like or dislike about each other and discuss shared future expectations. The questions to be explored are many, and rightfully so. Is the man or woman divorced? Does he or she have children from a previous relationship, and, if so, are they active in either parent's life? Is either person gainfully employed and, if so, in what type of work? Has either been raised by a single parent or were both parents in the home? What is each person's religious affiliation or is either of them an atheist?

Additionally, there is the question of intimate relations. How physical or intimate should a couple be when dating? The answer is different for every person. This is another time to account for religion. Many Christians take to heart Corinthians 6:19-20: "Don't you realize that your body is the temple of the Holy Spirit, who lives in you and was given to you by God? You do not belong to yourself, for God bought you with a high price. So you must honor God with your body."

Each of these questions, and many others, play a significant part in the success or failure of a relationship. Yet, we were not created to be alone; we were created for relationships. God stated this in Genesis 2:18, "Then the

Lord God said, 'It is not good for the man to be alone. I will make a helper who is just right for him.'"

However, the process of dating and its expected results will depend on where you and your partner are mentally, spiritually, physically, and even financially in your lives. It's important to recognize how these factors can affect your dating life together. Consider the following questions:

> <u>Mentally</u>: You and your partner may have a different perception regarding the status of your relationship. Are you both on one accord on the current state of your relationship and what the future of your relationship could or should look like?

> <u>Physically</u>: Is there a physical distance between you and your partner, i.e., is this a long-distance relationship? Is there an actual physical illness, disease, or impairment that creates challenges in the relationship?

> Spiritually: Do you share the same religious beliefs? If not, what type of challenges does that present in the relationship?
>
> Financially: What is the condition of your individual finances? Are you a saver or a spender? Do you utilize money as a tool or a weapon?

This is why communication is so important, even in the beginning stages of dating. If we consider marriage as the job, then dating would be the interview. During an interview, the employer seeks to discover whether the applicant has what it takes to become part of the organization. This can only be accomplished by asking pertinent and relevant questions about the candidate's background and future expectations.

In the context of dating, men and women should have the mindset of an interviewer. The goal of a couple should be to determine the expectations and boundaries in which they expect to operate in the relationship. Again, this should be done in the initial phase of getting to know one other in order to determine if dating exclusively is the right thing to do. We believe the purpose of dating is

Delayed Enlistment – Dating

to discover whether the other person might be a potential candidate for marriage. If one should discover the other person is not a good fit, at that point both should mutually agree to move on and not continue the relationship further.

As a military recruiter, it was common to have trainees in the Delayed Enlistment program for several months prior to their leaving for basic training. If at any time you discovered the trainee was not a good fit for the Air Force, then it was your duty and obligation to report your findings and remove the candidate from the program. Although this program is designed to acclimate recruits to military life, it is also designed to weed out recruits that might be potential liabilities down the road.

As couples continue their dating, they get a snapshot of what life would be like by spending time together. Is there a time limit on how long a couple should date before they decide on whether to take the next step? We believe that decision should be left up to each couple depending on their situation and circumstances. We certainly suggest couples have a conversation periodically about future expectations of the relationship and what the end game looks like. In other words, is marriage an option and, if so, how soon?

Having this conversation early and frequently can also avoid spending unnecessary years together dating only to find out later that your partner was never interested in getting married. How would this make you feel? Situations like this could actually become a doorway to feelings of resentment and bitterness on the part of the person hoping to be married; he or she might feel they've wasted a lot of their time with the wrong person. Sometimes a person might feel the other partner has taken advantage of him or her. This is why communication is key in the initial phase of dating. Both people can determine quickly if it's worth moving forward or moving on. (If you ever do find yourself in a situation where it is clear you must move on, the key is not to become bitter, angry, or resentful. These emotions will only stagnate you as well as delay or even prevent your personal growth and progress.)

In today's social media climate, finding the person right for you can be very challenging. It is often said our spouse should be our best friend, but how many of us can truthfully say this about the person we've married? My wife and I have truly become the best of friends, but not without that friendship being tested. Real friendships must be tested to reveal their authenticity.

In God's infinite wisdom, He has given us a blueprint for marriages through Jesus Christ, but without a true relationship with Him we are left to our own devices. This is why establishing a relationship with Christ should be a couple's first priority. "I am the vine, you are the branches. He who abides in Me, and I in him, bears much fruit, for without Me you can do nothing." (John 15:5) One of the very first marriages Christians learn about is the one between Christ and His bride, the church. Although this model should be the example of every Christian marriage, we can clearly see by the high divorce rate that it's not.

Just as we make the decision in marriage to surrender our lives to one another, our first surrendering should be to Jesus Christ. If you do not have a relationship with Christ, expectations and boundaries in a dating relationship can have a completely different meaning than what God has stated in His Word. Without God's blueprint for marriage, we are left to our own worldly devices to navigate how marriage is to be configured and carried out.

You can see this reflected in the state of marriage in the world today. People are defining what marriage is and is not. God's design for marriage is a covenant, not a contract; is heterosexual, not homosexual; and is monogamous, not polygamous. We need only to look to the scriptures to see the blueprint God has intended.

And the LORD God said, "*It is* not good that man should be alone; I will make him a helper comparable to him." Out of the ground the LORD God formed every beast of the field and every bird of the air and brought *them* to Adam to see what he would call them. And whatever Adam called each living creature, that *was* its name. So Adam gave names to all cattle, to the birds of the air, and to every beast of the field. But for Adam there was not found a helper comparable to him. And the LORD God caused a deep sleep to fall on Adam, and he slept; and He took one of his ribs, and closed up the flesh in its place. Then the rib which the LORD God had taken from man He made into a woman, and He brought her to the man. And Adam said: "This *is* now bone of my bones And flesh of my flesh; She shall be called Woman, Because she was taken out of Man." Therefore a man shall leave his father and mother and be joined to his wife, and they shall become one flesh. (Genesis 2:18-24)

> "You shall not lie with a male as with a woman. It *is* an abomination." (Lev. 18:22)

"Yet you say, 'For what reason?' Because the LORD has been witness Between you and the wife of your youth, With whom you have dealt treacherously; Yet she is your companion And your wife by covenant." (Mal. 2:14)

With that being said, if you have not truly surrendered your life to Jesus Christ, we would like to give you an opportunity to do so before going any further. We believe this is the most important decision anyone will ever make. The Bible says, "If you confess with your mouth the Lord Jesus and believe in your heart that God has raised Him from the dead, you will be saved. For with the heart one believes unto righteousness, and with the mouth confession is made unto salvation." (Rom. 10:9-10) If you have prayed this prayer, it's time to start communicating with the original architect of marriage,

Jesus Christ. Remember, too, John 15:5 quoted above, and ask the Lord to write this scripture on your heart lest we forget this important strategy.

2.

Basic Training/Boot Camp – The Engagement

Making the decision to spend the rest of one's life with another person in holy matrimony is a commitment not to be taken lightly. This decision should be preempted with much prayer and even fasting. Why? Because marriage is *meant* to be a lifelong commitment. Let me draw you back to our military analogy.

With the exception of those who have served in combat operations, basic military training, also known as boot camp, has to be one of the most challenging experiences a person can face. After completing the Delayed Enlistment program, military recruits are shipped off to their respective training facilities, or boot camps, to begin their military careers.

Boot camps can vary in length depending on the military branch. My wife and I can still recall the very first night we arrived at boot camp at Lackland Air Force Base, San Antonio, Texas. At that time, new recruits were called Rainbows because we represented every color and nationality. We had no resemblance of structure or order as a group, even down to the clothes we wore; everything was different. Little did we know we had a lot to learn and in the words of comedian Kevin Hart, "We gone learn today" what structure, order, and discipline was all about.

In the context of dating, a couple usually spends a lot of time just getting to know one another. Often, when one of them discovers something about the other person that might be awkward or annoying, he or she may overlook the issue as long as it's nothing harmful. However, once the individuals become engaged, their commitment to one another is solidified, and each should feel obligated to address any concerns that could be a potential problem for the relationship.

Basic Training/Boot Camp –The Engagement

You might ask what any of this has to do with basic military training. Just as an engagement signals to both parties another realm of commitment, basic military training does the same for the military recruit. The drill instructor is obligated to address any and all concerns he or she observes that could be an issue to the success of a recruit's career. Prior to joining the military, every decision the recruit made was probably always in his best interest. He controlled what he wore, what he ate, where he lived, where he worked, and who he associated with. In other words, the decisions the recruit made were mostly made without him having to consult with anyone.

This mentality quickly changes while going through boot camp. Every decision is now filtered through the lens of what's in the best interest of the military and/or service to our country. This lesson of sacrifice becomes one of the most important lessons learned during your military training. It is ingrained in every recruit from the time they first enlist until their separation or retirement from service.

In the same way recruits are taught the value and importance of sacrifice, the bible also speaks of this type of sacrifice in the book of Ephesians. Wives are instructed to submit themselves to their own husbands as to the Lord and husbands are to love their wives, just as Christ loved the church and died for it. These two pillars of sacrifice are critical to the success of any Christian marriage. God has given men and women unique roles in marriage based upon how He created us to thrive and function within this union. While men need to feel respected, women need to feel loved, and whenever these basic needs are not being met, the marriage is destined for problems.

Unfortunately, in marriages today, we see this all too often. Instead of men putting their wives first and vice versa, little if any consideration is given to how a decision might affect the other spouse. This sense of entitlement is rooted in pride and can hinder the couple from truly becoming one as the Bible speaks of in Mark 10:8, "and the two shall become one flesh."

How can we deal with the spirit of pride once we detect it? We must first acknowledge we have a pride issue and need help. During the days of Jesus's life on earth, He offered up prayers and petitions with fervent cries and

Basic Training/Boot Camp –The Engagement

tears to the One who could save Him from death, and He was heard because of His reverent submission. (Heb. 5:7) Second, we need to acknowledge and submit to God's sovereign authority with a humbling spirit, and He will give us strategies and plans on defeating our prideful ways. Finally, we must acknowledge and submit to the sovereign authority He has placed in our lives, whether it's in our jobs, our families, or our marriages. The key to overcoming pride is learning how-to walk-in humility.

A great example of this happened during my basic military training. It didn't take long for me and my compatriots to realize we were no longer in charge and a higher authority was now operating in our lives; our drill instructors. The faster we submitted to their authority, the better off we became. I won't say things got easier, however, our desire to conform and submit did.

Since most of you reading this book may not get an opportunity to serve in the military, God will have to use some other form of authority in your life to deal with your pride. My suggestion is to not fight it. Rather, embrace it and see the hand of God coming against your prideful spirit. We must always look to Jesus as our example. Although He was God, He humbled himself and took on the nature of a servant becoming obedient to the Father even unto death. (Phil. 2:6-8 modified) Know that God is a God of order and structure, and everything He does has an order and structure to it, including a couple's engagement. "He who finds a wife finds a good thing and obtains favor from the Lord." (Prov. 18:22)

Let me close this chapter by reminding you that an engagement is not just time to prepare for the wedding ceremony. It is, more importantly, time to prepare to become one together, as Jesus did with His bride, the church. While preparing for the joyous occasion can be exhilarating and even stressful, it should not overshadow the purpose of the ceremony. A couple cannot be so in love with the planning and wedding details that they forget the reason why they're having a wedding—to unite as one.

3.

Technical Training – Pre-Marital Counseling/Coaching

"...and in a multitude of counselors *there is* safety." (Prov. 24:6)

Every part of our lives requires some form of instruction, direction, leading, or guidance for us to operate and function in this world. We must learn "how to do" in order "to do".

After completing the basic military training course, each recruit is assigned to a technical training school. During this phase of training, the recruit learns the specific job he or she will continue throughout their respective careers. Technical training is task specific and geared toward teaching recruits how to effectively do their jobs. It's similar to a police officer attending the police academy. The training officer learns about riding patrols, manning security posts, guarding prisoners, riot controls, investigating cases, and many other law enforcement techniques. It only seems logical that each police officer would learn these critical techniques prior to working in the field, wouldn't you agree?

Would you also agree that in marriage, similar to a job, both parties now have new roles and responsibilities to learn? If you agree with this rationale, have you ever wondered why most married couples haven't taken the time to invest in pre-marital counseling or coaching? That can be a game changer in a relationship. According to Health Search Funding, couples who underwent counseling before their marriage had a 30% higher marital success rate than those who did not.

Counseling sessions give couples the opportunity to "open the hood and see what's going on with the engine" before making a commitment. Under the guidance of a professional, many important and often uncomfortable questions can be discussed openly in a safe environment. Questions like:

- How does your mate respond to you when you are vulnerable?
- In times of need, does your mate show compassion or empathy or are they condescending and righteous?
- Does your potential spouse want to have children?
- What are the "rules" of handling a disagreement?
- Is each partner familiar with credit or should they have a financial portfolio?

I would speculate most couples have very little dialogue, if any, concerning these very important questions. But, if this is truly the person you plan to spend the rest of your life with, you certainly owe it to yourself to know where they stand on important matters. Knowing this information early on in your relationship can give each of you an advantage on how to work through rough patches when something should arise. How can two walk together unless they agree? (Amos 3:3) This biblical principle should be foundational in a marriage.

Although we don't always agree on everything, we can exercise our right to disagree and not become stuck trying to convince the other person to change their position because they don't see it our way. For instance, my wife's professional background is in finance whereas mine has always been in law enforcement. She is more reserve with spending whereas I am just the opposite. We have decided in the best interest of our finances to have separate accounts for ourselves and a joint account for our bills. This decision alone has been beneficial to our finances as well as our marriage. Financial problems (money) are the second highest reason why couples get divorced. (Warren, S., (2019 Dec 13) 10 Most Common Reasons for Divorce, Marriage.com). Knowing this, we have incorporated financial strategies and principles into our marital counseling sessions to help guide couples into making better financial decisions. For some of our counselees, this is normally the first conversation they've had regarding their joint finances. Although they have become one in name, they are still very much divided financially. This is normally when we hear comments like, "I don't tell him how to spend his money and he doesn't tell me how to spend mine. I have my own money and pay my bills and he has his own money and pay his bills".

Why has this mentality become so common in marriages today? It's simple. People want to be in control. It's common to feel we need to have control over everything that happens in our life. We want to be in charge of our destiny without any outside assistance. We want to be able to dictate the course of our life without anyone's input.

This type of thinking is unrealistic as God is the Author and Finisher of the plans for our lives, including our marriages. Good marriages start with accountability and responsibility. All of us must be accountable, first and foremost, to God. "But first and most importantly seek (aim at, strive after) His kingdom and His righteousness [His way of doing and being right—the attitude and character of God], and all these things will be given to you also." (Matt. 6:33 AMP) His Word is the divinely inspired instruction manual for our lives. Secondly, we must be accountable to our spouses to truly build a marriage that is supportive of both people.

One of the principles recruits learn during Air Force technical training is that they are forever learning. The day we stop learning is the day we stop growing. We should make every effort to apply this same principle in our marriages. Pre-marital counseling is an excellent way to do this and create a firm foundation on which to build a marriage. This year my wife and I will celebrate thirty-one years of marriage, and we can honestly say we are still learning about one another. We both agree we're not the same as we were at age twenty, thirty, or even forty, so we must continue to give each other space and grace to grow.

We have attributed this commitment to forever learn about each other to the word of God as written in Romans 12:1-2, "I beseech you therefore by the mercies of Christ that you present your bodies a living sacrifice holy and acceptable to God which is your reasonable service, and be not conformed to this world but be ye transformed by the renewing of your mind that you may prove what is that good, acceptable and perfect will of God." By our mutual submission to God, we have allowed His voice to be the loudest in the room. His voice, the Word of God, becomes the ultimate authority on how we treat

Technical Training – Pre-Marital Counseling/Coaching

one another, how we respond to one another, and, most importantly, how we love one another as spelled out in the book of Ephesians.

The things that might have caused us stress during our younger years are now just reminders of how much the Word of God has changed and matured our thinking. Couples truly desiring to be wise in their relationships should start by asking the creator of wisdom, God, for guidance. "If any of you lacks wisdom, let him ask of God, who gives to all liberally and without reproach, and it will be given to him." (James 1:5)

There is a vast amount of resources and materials available to help strengthen and equip your marriage for success in addition to premarital counseling. I believe one of the best decisions my wife and I made in our marriage was to solicit help from seasoned married couples that we could model and learn from. These couples were often a part of the marriage ministry in the church we attended. We never imagined we would one day become the couple that God could use to bless someone else's marriage yet alone become authors of a book on the subject. "With man this is impossible, but with God all things are possible." (Matthew 19:26b)

4.

Commitment in Marriage

It is not a coincidence one of the very first counseling/coaching sessions we hold is on commitment. I can still recall the conversation the Lord had with me about commitment. In my prayer time the Lord revealed to me the importance of being committed to him above all else. "But seek first the kingdom of God and his righteousness, and all these other things would be added to you". (Matthew 6:33) As defined by Dictionary.com, commitment is an agreement or pledge to do something in the future; the state or an instance of being obligated or emotionally impelled. It is listed as a pledge; obligation; allegiance; dedication; loyalty; devotion; faithfulness; and fidelity on Thesaurus.com. Although a couple's love and commitment to one another must be at the core of their marriage, their commitment to God must be first and foremost.

Another word for commitment is vow. During a traditional marriage ceremony, couples normally recite vows to one another and to God. This is the most important part of the ceremony and probably the least understood. Here is what God says about making vows: "He has no pleasure in fools; fulfill your vow." (Eccles. 5:4) When you make a vow to God, do not delay to fulfill it.

Remember how we promised God we're going to love our spouses for better or for worse, richer or poorer, in sickness and in health? If that were true of everyone and people truly meant what they said, we probably wouldn't have a divorce rate as high as it is. We make these promises because we like how they sound, not truly understanding what it might cost us down the road. There have been many challenges in our marriage that could have justified us getting divorced but we both agreed not to give up. No matter how bad things got, we simply weren't getting divorced.

Commitment in Marriage

In our eyes, we were both soldiers and if the military had taught us anything, it was how not to quit. We were going to love one another through the darkest of times because that is what we agreed to. Looking back over our military careers, we both recall doing things we felt we hadn't signed up for, but because we said yes, we considered them as just another sacrifice that came with the job. In the same vein, we were going to be as committed to our marriage as we were to serving our country.

This display of commitment is rooted in agape (unconditional) love. This type of love is what God expects from each of us, and we can achieve it because we are created in His image and His likeness. Love never gives up, never loses faith, is always hopeful, and endures through every circumstance. (1 Cor. 13:7) This type of sacrificial love is rooted and grounded in commitment and can only be accomplished, in our opinion, through God.

If we want to strengthen our commitment to our spouses, we must first strengthen our commitment to God. This is one of the most valuable lessons about commitment God taught me. He let me know I would never be committed to my marriage, my children, or anything else if I was not committed to Him first. God is a God of order, and when our priorities are off, everything else is too.

Commitment in marriage takes time and sacrifice. Both the husband and wife should be in it for the long haul, seeking to make the union enduring, and not running away or quitting when things get tough or the relationship is tested. There is truth in the saying, "anything worth having is worth fighting for." Marriage should not be entered into with the mindset of "if it gets hard, or we grow apart, or we can't seem to agree, we can get a divorce." It takes faith and resolve to stay committed to each other and fight for what God has joined.

Here are some practical steps couples can take to create a solid foundation for their marriage. First, establish a vision for your marriage. We highly suggest both spouses seek God in prayer and petition Him about having a vision for your marriage (what it should look like). Jesus gave us a great example when He said:

Husbands, love your wives, just as Christ loved the church and gave himself up for her to make her holy, cleansing her by washing with water through the word, and to present her to himself as a radiant church, without stain or wrinkle or any other blemish, but holy and blameless. (Ephesians 5:25-27)

Wow! Just imagine if men really took this scripture to heart and began to love their wives as Christ loved the church. I can hear men saying now, "Why does it have to be me? She doesn't appreciate it or reciprocate it." They may even offer some other excuse. My response is simple. As the husband, because you have been called to lead, you set the example. As the priest of your home, you establish the order and create the culture for your family. In other words, the vision for your family should start with the priest, you! Where there is no vision, the people perish. (Prov. 29:18)

Secondly, we must begin to speak differently about our marriages. One of the tenants of Christianity is faith. Faith is seeing and believing things before they manifest. (Heb. 11:1 modified) This step becomes critical to the success of your marriage. What you say and think about your marriage becomes your reality. "As a man thinks in his heart, so is he." (Prov. 23:7)

My wife and I had to stop making excuses for why our marriage was failing and begin to take ownership of what we had both allowed to take place. The Word of God tells us that we will have trials and tribulations in this world, which includes in our marriage. It should not come as a surprise when we experience trouble in our union on any level. The key to understanding and successfully overcoming marital trials and tribulations is God's word and your commitment to one another. In marriage, you are no longer two but one flesh. Therefore, what God has joined together let no man separate. (Matt. 19:6)

Remaining steadfast in commitment was one of the first lessons God taught my wife and I while we were going through marital difficulties. Instead of allowing the difficulty to pull us apart, we both agreed we would pray about it and discuss it during our leisurely Sunday walks together. This normally gave us time to consider our position and allow the Lord to give us wisdom on how we could move forward. As we put our trust and confidence in God, and not ourselves, we soon found things to work out much easier.

Commitment in Marriage

We quickly noticed that our old way of handling difficulties was certainly not the answer. In the past, whenever we disagreed about a situation, we would spend the next few days upset not communicating. This only led to feelings of anger, bitterness and resentment towards one another—feelings that over time could have eroded our marriage.

Hopefully, since you are reading this book, you are already willing to put forth the work required to turn things around in your marriage. First, we want you to take personal responsibility to renew your commitment to God because without His wisdom and guidance, you're left to your own understanding to figure things out (that probably hasn't worked out too well). With your commitment to God, start by spending quality time with Him. What does that look like? Although each person is different it should include reading His Word, praying, fasting, and eventually making yourself available and attending/serving in a local church. Jesus said, "I must be about my Father's business." (Luke 2:49) We too must be about what God has called us to do. As each spouse begins to purposefully pursue the things of God, He will make each aware of the special gifts and talents

He individually has blessed them with, gifts and talents they can readily make available to each other as well as the rest of the world.

After renewing your commitment to God, each person must ask for forgiveness from God and one another. This step is crucial for letting go of the past and moving forward in your purpose. "But if you do not forgive others their sins, your father will not forgive your sins." (Matt. 6:15) When we fail to forgive each other, we essentially force God's hand not to forgive us.

As you begin to walk in forgiveness, you literally begin to tear down every wall you've erected that has separated you from hearing and obeying God. When my wife and I reached this step, one of our prayers was, "Lord, help us to see each other as You do." If God can still love us in spite of our flaws and shortcomings, surely, we can love each other.

During this time of forgiveness, it's important that you seek to resolve any and all unresolved conflicts. This is not the time to justify your wrong doings or even attempt to cover them. Each person must keep in mind it's not

Commitment in Marriage

about who's right or wrong, or who's winning or losing; it is about remaining together. How a couple handles this process is what matters to the marriage. While God did declare "the two shall become one," He didn't promise becoming one wouldn't have its challenges. But it is important, as husband and wife, for a couple to remain unified, even in times of disagreement.

Finally, we strongly suggest couples start verbalizing their commitment to one another by praying together daily. One of the first things my wife and I noticed about praying together every day was how much closer it brought us. If there was a time that we found ourselves upset with one another, before we began to pray about it, the Lord would reveal it and gently unction us to resolve it. "Therefore, if you are offering your gift at the altar and there remember that your brother or sister has something against you, leave your gift there before the altar and go. First be reconciled to them, and then come and offer your gift." (Matt. 5:23-24)

In other words, before you offer your prayers to God, first be sure your heart is right and you're not holding offense against someone. This is one of the reasons a lot of our prayers are hindered because we have avoided dealing with our unresolved issues and still think we can have an audience with God. Since we know God is a God of order, lets resolve our issues first and then lift one another up in prayer. Remember, a family that prays together stays together.

5.

Communication in Marriage

One of the keys to a healthy and successful marriage is strong communication. A couple's ability to communicate with one another, and with God, is crucially related to the life or death of their marriage. "The tongue has the power of life and death and those who love it will eat its fruit." (Prov. 18:21) We should not forget, because we are created in the image and likeness of God, that He has given us the power to create or to destroy with our words.

Communication can be difficult, marriage notwithstanding, because everyone comes from different backgrounds, has different experiences, and is exposed to different cultures. All this affects how we communicate with one another, both in what we say and how we say it to how we interpret what's said to us.

For example, since my mother and father were divorced when I was born, I never experienced a relationship with my father whereas my wife, on the other hand, had to deal with the grief of losing her father at an early age and being raised by her mother and grandmother. Both experiences impacted how my wife and I viewed the different roles of a husband and wife in a marriage.

Also, I was the youngest in my family whereas my wife was the oldest of her siblings. I had become accustomed to someone taking care of me whereas my wife had the responsibility of taking care of her siblings. We both had very different childhood experiences and it was through those experiences that we were now attempting to raise children of our own. I can finally admit, I had no idea what I was doing. Remember, I was the youngest, so I wasn't responsible for anyone except myself and that was even a challenge. On the other hand, my wife being the oldest in her family had experience raising children, so she was well prepared. Thank God we had each other. "Two are better than one, because they have a good return

Communication in Marriage

for their labor: If either of them falls down, one can help the other up. But pity anyone who falls and has no one to help them up." (Eccles. 4:9-10)

Thankfully, effective communication is a skill that can be learned and practiced in order to build a successful marriage. The ability to speak honestly, listen with intention, and understand with compassion is essential between a husband and wife. Although we learn a lot about communication in the educational system, we can learn a great deal more through the Word of God. God is a master communicator and the originator of all languages. When God created the heavens and the earth, He but only had to speak it into creation. As Christians, we also understand that whatever God says comes to pass, and, since we're created in the image and likeness of God, we must guard what we say.

James, the brother of Jesus, taught that even though the tongue is a small member of the body, it controls the body. It guides the body like the bit in a horse's mouth or the rudder on a ship. (James 3:1-6) By our words, we can develop a healthy and vibrant marriage that ultimately glorifies God or a dysfunctional and cancerous one that eventually comes to ruin.

One of the ways we can learn to communicate better with our spouses is by spending quality time together. Think back to the time you first started dating your spouse. How much time did you try to spend together? How much of that time did you spend arguing or disagreeing about something? Most likely, you spent more time in positive and loving conversation than in hurtful, disruptive talk. When a person truly cares about someone, he or she invests the necessary time getting to know that person. This shouldn't stop after the dating is done.

My wife and I were married over thirty years ago, and I don't believe we could have lasted this long without learning how to communicate with one another and, more importantly, learning how to listen. Listening is one of most neglected aspects of communication. Given that God gave us two ears and one mouth, we should try to spend more time listening and less time talking. One of the concerns we normally hear while counseling couples is that they're not listening to one another. It is imperative for the growth and health of a marriage that

Communication in Marriage

husbands and wives' study and learn the communication style of their spouses. While their styles may be different, they should complement each other.

Listening truly is an art, and it helps to practice it if you're going to get better at it. In order to learn how your spouse communicates, you <u>must</u> learn to listen to understand. The time to learn to listen is not when you're tired, consumed with work or the kids, or in the midst of a heated disagreement. The best time is when you and your spouse are spending quality time together in a place where you can discuss your emotions and feelings and have each other's undivided attention. It's during this time that you can sincerely listen and focus on what your spouse is saying, both verbally and non-verbally. Of all the people in the world, the one person you should be able to be the most vulnerable and transparent with is your spouse.

One of the ways to improve your listening skills as a couple is by repeating back what you've just heard from your spouse for clarification. This will accomplish two things. First, it ensures you've each heard the conversation correctly, but, more importantly, it lets your spouse know you're listening to them. Begin by positioning yourself to hear what your spouse is saying. Then agree each spouse can speak freely without fear of shame, guilt, or condemnation. After one of you speaks, practice listening by repeating back what was said for a clear understanding. This way your spouse can verify what he or she said and what you heard is correct. This alone will cut down on the stress, strife, and animosity that could happen when you speak with each other. Plus, the extra moment of gaining clarification will allow you time to respond more effectively.

Practicing this listening skill will keep you both from falling into what we call the "double–dutch trap." This is when a person is listening to respond instead of listening to understand. That person is so busy waiting to jump in and get his or her point across that he or she fails to listen to what was just said. It becomes a never-ending cycle, much like that jump rope just twirling as someone waits to jump in.

The "double-dutch trap" frequently happens when a person feels that what he or she has to say is more important than the other person. It also happens when someone believes what he or she is saying is right and the other person is wrong. Can you see how there is no winner in this situation, and especially not for the marriage? God is not getting the glory.

Another way for husbands and wives to help improve their communication is to watch for nonverbal cues. Many times, there is more communicated by what a person is not saying than by what is actually said. This is something a good spouse will learn to discern. Study your spouse's body language and tendencies in order to enhance communication. Are they attentive and alert or withdrawn and tense regarding something? Have you noticed a tone or pitch change in their voice? Did you hear the sigh in their breath? Did they cross their legs or arms as if they're not open to it?

These are all telltale signs of concerns our spouse is feeling that we must learn to discern. An example might be something as simple as a wife asking a husband his opinion about an outfit she'd like to purchase. Instead of the husband being open and honest about his opinion, he chooses to remain neutral and shrugs his shoulders. This type of nonverbal communication can mean a host of things that can be very confusing to his spouse. Is he saying he doesn't know, doesn't care, not interested, not sure, how much does it cost, we don't have the money for it, you don't need it, need time to think about it or that he just doesn't have an opinion? If you're thinking one of these answers than you're probably just as confused as his wife. Can you see where this type of communication can lead to conflict and or misunderstandings?

With time, patience, and practice, you and your spouse can learn to improve your communication as well as other areas in your marriage. We truly believe communication principles and strategies can be strengthened in marriage when both parties are walking closely with their Savior and abiding in His presence. When you remain in Christ, God will give you the fruits needed to be successful. These fruits include patience, self-control, love, forgiveness, and even the right words to say. Jesus said, "I am the vine; you are the branches. If a man remains in me and I in him, he will bear much fruit; apart from me you can do nothing." (John 15:5)

6.

Gender Roles in Marriage

> "And the Lord God said, '*It is* not good that man should be alone; I will make him a helper comparable to him.'" (Gen. 2:18)

The Bible is God's Word for every area of our lives. It identifies every role in our lives, from the womb to the tomb and on to eternity. In order to live holy and righteous, we must follow the instructions He has laid out in His Word. "Because it is written, be ye holy; for I am holy." (1 Peter 1:16) When we don't follow His Word, we find ourselves going through various trials and tribulations that could have been avoided. God designed marriage, and when people do not follow His design, their marriage is destined for problems.

In the book of Genesis, God said it was not good for man to be alone so He created for him a suitable helper—woman. As the original architect for marriage, it was God who established the roles for both the husband and the wife. The apostle Paul used the story of creation as justification for a man having authority and leadership over his wife. "I do not permit a woman to teach or to have authority over a man, she must be silent. For Adam was formed first, then Eve." (1 Tim. 2:12-13) He further referenced that God gave Adam the authority to name his wife, the woman He had just created. In the ancient culture, birth order was very important. It showed one's rank. Paul said God's creation of Adam first was not haphazard, but done by sovereign design. It was meant to show his leadership and authority in relation to his wife.

God is a God of order. He understood the institution of marriage could not function properly if it did not have clear leadership. This is true with any institution: the military, business, school, even the church. During our military basic training we learned the importance of the chain of command. The success and or failure of any organization will always be influenced by the chain of command or lack thereof. "Let every person be subject

Gender Roles in Marriage

to the governing authorities. For there is no authority except from God, and those that exist have been instituted by God. Therefore, whoever resists the authorities resists what God has appointed, and those who resist will incur judgement." (Romans 13:1-2) God expects order not just in the workplace but also in the family. Therefore, God intended for the husband to be the leader in order to achieve His original purposes through marriage.

With that said, what should the husband's leadership look like practically? What should the wife's submission look like? The husband is not supposed to be a dominate tyrant, and the wife is not called to be a doormat. Instead of using his leadership to control or dominate his wife, God calls the husband to use his leadership to love his wife. God planned this from the beginning. The husband would lead through loving his wife.

> Husbands, love your wives, just as Christ loved the church and gave himself up for her to make her holy, cleansing her by the washing with water through the word, and to present her to himself as a radiant church, without stain or wrinkle or any other blemish, but holy and blameless.

> In this same way, husbands ought to love their wives as their own bodies. He who loves his wife loves himself. (Eph 5:25-28)

This type of sacrificial love and submission can only be achieved through the grace of God by way of the Holy Spirit.

Now, let's discuss the role of the wife. Remember, it was God who stated man should not be alone and that he would need help. The role of a wife has always been to help and assist her husband. You might be thinking, "Help and assist in what?" Using our marriage as an example, my wife has been instrumental in every aspect of my life. I would not be the man I am today had it not been for the love, prayers, and sacrifice of my wife.

Consider the honor given to Sarah because of the way she submitted to her husband, Abraham. The Bible says, "For this is the way the holy women of the past who put their hope in God used to make themselves beautiful. They were submissive to their own husbands, like Sarah, who obeyed Abraham and called him her master. You are her daughters if you do what is right and do not give way

Gender Roles in Marriage

to fear." (1 Pet. 3:5-6) Sarah called her husband master, and Scripture says this is one of the characteristics that makes a woman beautiful to the Lord. A woman considering marriage today should ask herself, "Am I ready to honor and submit to my husband as unto the Lord? Am I willing to submit to his plans as he hears from God?"

God's design for marriage is clearly defined, and the role of husband and wife are plainly stated. So why do married couples have such a difficult time with their roles? If we are honest, no one likes to be controlled or made to feel less than anyone else. Our constitution reminds us that we were are all created equal so why should anyone be made to feel subservient, even in marriage?

Early on in our marriage, my wife and I always seemed to compete against one another. The fact we were both military didn't seem to help; we were similar in rank and normally had to compete against one another for promotion. Although we didn't say it consciously, we were both also competing for control of our marriage. The Bible speaks about this type of behavior in Genesis 3:16, "Your desire will be for your husband and he will rule over you." In other words, the wife will attempt to control the husband and husband will try to rule and lord over the wife. God's design for marriage is not for us to be in competition with one another, however, until we learn and accept our specific roles as He's established, this can be the result.

So, how does a person learn what a husband or wife is supposed to be if it was never modeled before them? And, even if a person had an example of a marriage in his or her life, did it show true signs of love, honor and respect between the spouses, or did it show signs of what the world defines a marriage should look like? When looking for what defines a husband, a wife, and a Christian marriage, we need look no further than the source of all things created in heaven and earth—God's Word.

Years ago, marital roles within the home were distinctly defined. You might recall the traditional roles. The husband was to be the bread winner for the family; the wife was to stay home, cook and clean, and raise the children. While there are still households that operate in this traditional fashion, there are many that are far from it. It is okay to define the male and female household

Gender Roles in Marriage

responsibilities as different from what they have been. Determining who does laundry, who cleans the house, who maintains the lawn, etc. are merely decisions about tasks. Who does a chore or earns a paycheck does not change God's roles for a husband and wife?

As a husband, your priorities should be your relationship with God, then family, then work. Your main roles are to be the priest of your home and to love your wife as commanded in scripture. As a wife, your priorities should be your relationship with God, then family, then work. Your role is to be a help mate and to respect your husband. The way in which a couple carries out these roles are to be rooted in love. Each person's love for Christ and His commands should be the driving force to carry out His mandate as it relates to marriage.

> Love is patient and kind; love does not envy or boast; it is not arrogant or rude. It does not insist on its own way; it is not irritable or resentful; it does not rejoice at wrongdoing but rejoices with the truth. Love bears all things, believes all things, hopes all things, endures all things. Love never ends. (1 Cor. 13:1-8)

As couples begin to follow the instructions God has outlined in his word concerning their respective roles in marriage get ready to see the Lord fight their battles and strengthen their marriage for his glory. "For the eyes of the Lord run to and fro throughout the whole earth, to give strong support to those whose heart is blameless toward him." (2 Chronicles 16:9)

7.

Conflict in Marriage

Every marriage will experience some form of conflict. Some of you reading this now might be thinking, "Not my marriage." Yes, your marriage too; no marriage is immune. Conflict is essentially a part of human nature. After Adam sinned in the Garden, conflict ensued. When God asked him if he had eaten of the forbidden tree, he did not simply say, "Yes." He said, "The woman you gave me, gave me the fruit and I did eat." (Gen. 3:12) He indirectly blamed God and directly blamed the woman. The woman then blamed the serpent.

So, when sin entered the world, so did conflict. In fact, God said one of the results of sin would be conflict between the man and the woman. The wife would desire to control the husband and the husband would try to dominate the woman by force. (Gen. 3:16) The apostle Paul taught one of the fruits of the flesh, our sin nature, is discord. (Gal. 5:20) We are prone to offend others, to be offended, to hate, to withhold forgiveness, and to divide. Sadly, these fruits are prone to occur within the marriage union. Couples should be aware of this, and therefore prepare to resolve conflict in marriage.

Conflict in marriage can sometimes feel like a game of tug-of-war with each side using all the strength they have to pull the other to their side while resisting being pulled themselves. The pull of the back and forth is not a good feeling personally and it's not good for a marriage. Conflict can be harmful or even disastrous for a marriage if it is not handled in a timely manner and or without care and compassion. Allowing conflict to remain unresolved can drive a wedge between spouses that drives them further away from each other. It is vitally important to understand that your spouse is not your enemy. "Can two walk together, unless they are agreed?" (Amos 3:3) A great marriage consist of harmony, unity and most importantly agreement.

Conflict in Marriage

It's important to have the right attitude when resolving conflict. Conflict, as with all trials, is meant to test our faith, reveal sin in our hearts, develop character, and draw us closer to God. Paul stated this: "Not only so, but we also rejoice in our sufferings, because we know that suffering produces perseverance; perseverance character; and character, hope." (Rom. 5:3-4) Similarly, James said, "Consider it pure joy, my brothers, whenever you face trials of many kinds, because you know that the testing of your faith develops perseverance." (James 1:2-3)

So, Paul said we should rejoice in sufferings, and James said we should consider it "pure joy" when we encounter them because of God's purposes in them. God does not waste suffering, including conflict within marriage. God uses conflict to make us grow into the image of Christ, which should be our ultimate goal. Many times, God uses our spouse as sand paper to smooth out areas in our life that don't reflect Christ. It has often been said, "Marriage is not about happiness; it is about holiness. And when we are holy, then we will truly be happy." (Thomas, G. *Sacred Marriage*.)

In marriage, people enter the ultimate accountability relationship, which is meant to help them grow as God's children. In marital conflict, couples must develop perseverance so they can produce the fruits God wants to cultivate in their marriage. This is difficult because the natural response to trials and conflict is to bail or quit. And that's what many couples do. At some point they say, "That's enough. I can't live like this," and they quit. Some do this by divorcing, others by distancing themselves emotionally and physically as they stop working to fix the marriage.

However, Scripture teaches us to persevere in trials, which includes conflict. The word persevere means to "bear up under a heavy weight." God matures us individually and corporately as we bear up under the heavy weight. He teaches us to trust Him more. He helps us develop peace, patience, and joy, regardless of our circumstances. He helps us grow in character as we "let perseverance finish its work." (James 1:4)

In order to resolve conflict, we must develop perseverance. That's essentially what we promised to do in our wedding vows. We committed to love our spouse in sickness and in health, for better or for worse. We should be thankful when it is "better" and persevere when it is "worse." For those who do, there is fruit. Paul said, "Let us not become weary in doing good, for at the proper time we will reap a harvest if we do not give up." (Gal. 6:9)

Additionally, not only must people have the right attitude when encountering conflict, they also must sow the right seeds to resolve it. Paul said whatever we sow, we will also reap. (Gal. 6:7) Sowing and reaping is a principle God set throughout the earth, and it is at work within every marriage as well. If couples sow negative seeds, they will reap negative fruit.

Sadly, even though couples all want a positive harvest in their marriage, they typically respond in ways that are counter to that. A wife wants her husband to spend more time with her, but in order to get that, she criticizes him. The fruit she desires is opposite of the seed she is sowing. The seed of criticism will only produce a negative fruit in her husband. Similarly, a husband who wants intimacy with his wife actually begins to withdraw from her. He withdraws hoping that this will draw her closer, but it actually does the opposite. The negative seed of withdrawing cannot produce the positive fruit of intimacy.

In conflict, people must do the opposite of what their nature desires. We may have a desire to raise our voice and/or to hurt the other person, but these seeds will only produce negative fruit and potentially destruction of the marriage. To resolve conflict, we must always sow the right seeds. Similarly, consider what Paul taught about how each of us should respond to an enemy. He said:

> Do not take revenge, my friends, but leave room for God's wrath, for it is written: "It is mine to avenge; I will repay," says the Lord. On the contrary: "If your enemy is hungry, feed him; if he is thirsty, give him something to drink. In doing this, you will heap burning coals on his head." Do not be overcome by evil but overcome evil with good. (Rom. 12:19-21)

What Paul is saying is, that in response to an enemy, we must overcome evil with good. Instead of responding with anger or seeking revenge, we should sow kindness and generosity. If our enemy is hungry, feed him. If he is thirsty, give him something to drink. Instead of being overcome by evil, we must overcome evil by continually sowing good seeds.

So, what good seeds can we sow when we are experiencing conflict in our marriage? Maybe it could be the good seed of a listening ear. It could be the seed of affirmation. It could be the seed of service. Certainly, it must be the seed of unconditional love. In conflict, we must sow good seeds to reap a good harvest.

With that said, we must always remember that conflict resolution is very much like farming. Sometimes, it may take months or years to get the harvest we desire. Many become discouraged while waiting for their spouse to change or for the conflict to be resolved. Typically, in that discouragement, people start to sow negative seeds that only hinder the harvest they seek. A verse worth repeating while considering conflict resolution is, "Let us not become weary in doing good, for at the proper time we will reap a harvest if we do not give up." (Gal. 6:9)

Another important principle to apply in marriage conflict is talking to our spouse first before talking to anybody else. This is a principle Christ taught about dealing with sin in general. He said, "If your brother sins against you, go and show him his fault, just between the two of you. If he listens to you, you have won your brother over." (Matt. 18:15) This is important for several reasons. First, it shows respect for our spouse. It is disrespectful to discuss a problem with our mom, our friend, or anybody else. If our spouse finds out, it may actually cause more conflict.

Secondly, every story has two sides, and those who are closest to us, such as family and friends, may not have the ability to give us unbiased counsel. This does not mean that we shouldn't talk to those closest to us, we should, but only after trying to resolve it with our spouse first. And when we do talk to others, we should still respect and honor our spouse.

My wife and I might not always agree on something; however, we've learned not to allow our disagreements to divide us. We can agree to disagree and still have unity and love in our marriage. I can still recall having a discussion with God about an issue in my marriage and the Lord asked me, "Do you want to be right or do you want to be married?" As much as I pressed the Lord for a third option, it became apparent these were my only two options available. My desire to be right would come at a great price and I decided it wasn't worth losing my marriage over it. Neither should you in a similar situation. I have learned to pick and choose my battles, because every battle is not meant to be fought. Sometimes you must lose a few battles to win the war. "Understand this, my dear brothers and sisters: You must all be quick to listen, slow to speak, and slow to get angry." (James 1:19)

Arguing, fussing, heated debate, or whatever you call conflict can be resolved in a civil manner. Learn to fight fair (Fighting in this context meaning expressing disagreement or anger; it does not mean causing another physical harm). No one knows how to hit us below the belt like our spouse, right? Putting rules in place for conflict can help spouses avoid hurling insults and accusations that purposely wound or shame the other spouse or cause damage the marriage may not be able to recover from. The goal is to get to the root of the conflict. While conflict is not a pleasant or comfortable space to be in, it is not always bad.

How do you fight fair? Agree to set boundaries in place:

- Stay calm and maintain control of yourself
- Don't raise your voice
- No yelling
- Do not interrupt each other when speaking
- Listen to understand, not to respond
- Watch your body language as you listen
- Don't bring up past issues
- Focus on the current situation
- Learn to forgive
- Don't criticize
- No name calling or using bad language
- No blaming or lashing out
- Apologize
- Take responsibility for hurting your spouse
- Be accountable

These communication techniques can transform your marriage, drawing you closer together to each other.

The next time you encounter a conflict in your marriage, put the steps for fighting fair and setting boundaries to use. You may be surprised how effective the process can be. If it gets to the point where you've tried and nothing seems to work, seek outside help. Marriage counseling is not a bad word. There are numerous professionals (Christian and non-Christian) in this field who can provide you the tools you need to help your marriage. "Where no counsel is, the people fail: but in the multitude of counselors there is safety." (Proverbs 11:14)

8.

Financial Faithfulness in Marriage

"The earth is the LORD's, and everything in it,
the world, and all who live in it." (Ps. 24:1)

I started this lesson with the word of God for a reason. This is probably one of the most controversial subjects amongst congregants in the Christian church. Although most churches teach and expect their members to tithe and give offerings, less than 20% of their members actually do.

When petitioned about not tithing, normally the response is, "Tithing was under the law, and we are now under grace" or "Tithing was only in the Old Testament." Jesus warned the Pharisee's in the book of Luke 11:42, "Woe to you Pharisees, because you give God a tenth of your mint, rue and all other kinds of garden herbs, but you neglect justice and the love of God. You should have practiced the latter without leaving the former undone." This scripture clearly refutes the notion of tithing only being in the Old Testament and that Jesus somehow did away with it. Jesus said, "Do not think that I have come to abolish the Law or the Prophets; I have not come to abolish them but to fulfill them." (Matt. 5:17)

We live in a society and culture today where most people don't take kindly to being told what to do, especially not with their money. In our experience, we have found money and possessions can rip a marriage apart almost as fast as infidelity can. Jesus dealt with this exact issue during His ministry on earth, recounted in Matthew 19:16-22. There was a rich young ruler who asked Jesus what good thing he could do to obtain eternal life. Jesus, knowing the man's heart, told him to keep the commandments. The man replied, "I have kept them all from my youth." Jesus finally tells the man if he'd like to be perfect, he should sell all that he has, give the money to the poor, and then follow Him; then he will have treasure in heaven. When the man heard this, he went away grieved because he owned so much and treasured his possessions more than a relationship with Christ.

We believe this story gets to the heart of the matter. Just as the rich young ruler saw his possessions as belonging to him, often people see their possessions as belonging to themselves only. They think of them in terms of "my money, my house, my car, my children, my clothes, my time....my, my, my." If everything belongs to you, then the next logical question is what belongs to God? If you truly believe the Word of God and you understand everything belongs to Him according to Psalms 24:1, then you must accept you are only a steward over what He has given you, including your money. Imagine how different things would be if we embraced this concept of stewardship?

When asked to sacrifice his only son, Abraham obeyed God and was blessed beyond measure. The enemy, Satan, knows as long as we covet our possessions our hearts remain loyal to them and not to Christ. "For where your treasure is, there will your heart be also." (Matt.

6:21) If I were a betting man, I would say embracing this kingdom mindset is probably the second biggest challenge for Christians today. Most of us have never lived in a government ruled by a king so this way of thinking is foreign to us. Dr. Myles Monroe was the first preacher I ever heard preach a sermon about the kingdom. He said, "In a kingdom, the king owns everything so nothing belongs to you and since nothing belongs to you, it is the king's responsibility to provide everything you need." If Jesus Christ is our Lord and King and He warns us not to worry about such things as clothing, food, and shelter, then we must trust He will provide them as promised in Matthew 6:25-34.

God is the creator of all things. Therefore, He is the owner of all things, not us. We are merely stewards over what He has entrusted us to manage. And, since everything belongs to God, we are not to be negligent or irresponsible with His resources. We are to act responsibly with the care and upkeep of the property, personal possessions, and money He has blessed us with. Just as God has a plan for marriage, He has a plan for how we manage and utilize our finances. Our finances are a resource meant to be a blessing to God's people. Remember, ALL things

Financial Faithfulness in Marriage

belong to God, even our finances. The misunderstanding of this fact is how people get themselves into financial stress, financial misuse, and financial unfaithfulness.

The more my wife and I embraced stewardship and not ownership, the more we have seen how God has been able to use us. Our jobs have become a place where Christ uses us to minister the gospel. Our home is another place where the love of Christ can shelter those who needed it. Our cars have become mere transportation to accomplish His will. Our money is just another resource He can use to further the gospel and build His kingdom. Our time is used to glorify God and to serve others.

This is how Jesus uses His children to fulfill the great commission and spread the gospel as outlined in Matthew 28:16-20. If we are going to truly be about His business, then the first order of business is to view ourselves in service to our Savior. The Bible says no man can serve two masters; either he'll love the one and hate the other (Matt. 6:24). Therefore, we can't serve both God and money.

How we manage our finances becomes a litmus test of how we manage souls. Those who are faithful with money can be trusted with leading people, training them, caring for them, etc. This is part of the reason God requires elders to not love money and to run their own household well (1 Tim. 3:3-4). Running one's household well includes faithfulness with finances. If a person is unfaithful with finances, he will be an unfaithful steward of people. However, when one is faithful with finances, God can entrust him with discipleship opportunities. "For exaltation *comes* neither from the east nor from the west nor from the south. But God *is* the Judge: He puts down one and exalts another." (Ps. 75:6-7)

The bottom line is spreading the gospel costs money, and we should want to give to help spread it. God promises to give grace to meet all the needs of cheerful givers. God will make "all grace abound" so those who follow Him will have all they need (2 Cor. 9:7-8). I believe many marriages struggle with lack today simply because couples are not faithful givers. "Then he said, 'Beware! Guard against every kind of greed. Life is not measured by how much you own.'" (Luke 12:15)

Financial Faithfulness in Marriage

Financial stress is one of the top reasons for conflict in marriage and divorce. Financial woes can tear a marriage and family apart. It was never God's will for finances to be a source of discord. It is His will for finances to be a blessing and a source of overflowing grace in a marriage. Therefore, to reap the benefits of God's blessings, couples need to understand and follow God's plan for finances. Giving is a sacrifice. It is God's desire that we give in order to advance the kingdom of God. We do this by spreading His gospel and in giving financially. However, we must first surrender our lives to the Lord. If we cannot surrender our lives freely unto Him, how can we in turn give of our finances or anything else in our lives to Him freely?

The key to being faithful with finances is not to love money. Money can be a thief. It can steal the hearts and minds of a husband, a wife, or both in the marriage. The Word says "God loves a cheerful giver." Many marriages have financial strife simply because couples choose not to be faithful givers. As a result, they bring a curse upon their finances.

The desire to obtain earthly wealth and success can draw spouses away from the Lord, which tears a marriage apart. For example, a husband may work extra-long hours at work for overtime pay, which unfortunately keeps him from spending quality time with his family. A wife may spend many hours after work networking and taking on extra work in order to get a promotion, also neglecting time with family.

Money and material possessions in themselves are not a bad thing. However, when it comes to money, people must look at the condition of their own heart. Husbands and wives should examine themselves individually and as a couple. Do both give willingly unto the Lord or are their thoughts and behaviors divided?

Money answers many things, but it should not be master over our lives and marriages. Money is a subject that should be covered in pre-marital counseling and during the course of your marriage. If a couple is not already aware of the fact, this will identify which person is gifted in money management as well as who is the spender and who is the saver. Discussing finances and the use of money is crucially important for couples. For example, it is prudent for couples to invest and save for emergencies, their kids, education, etc. It is also important to be unified on how family money will be spent.

Be mindful. Wealth and riches can be deceptive. The pursuit of it, while good, can pull a person away from his or her spouse and family if they become obsessed with it. Couples can spend their whole lives trying to obtain more, thinking they will be satisfied with material things, but, in the end, they only will be left unsatisfied. Money can promote pride in people when they have it and insecurity when they lack it. Do not allow money to master your marriage. "For the love of money is the root of all evil." (1 Tim. 6:10a)

9.

Raising Godly Children

The only perfect model of parenting is God the Father. Therefore, as we look at Him and His Word, we can discern principles about raising godly children. Raising children can be the most challenging, yet the most rewarding job a parent will ever have. We say challenging because, just as we are being corrected and chastened by God our Father, we in turn are attempting to do the same to our children, and we don't always get it right.

> "Train up a child in the way he should go, and when he is old he will not depart from it." (Prov. 22:6)

The Lord is so gracious; He gives you what you need even when you don't realize you need it. Children are a blessing from God. Being entrusted to nurture, guide, and care for them is an enormous task. Regardless of who we are, what we do, or where we're from, raising children requires help. There are many books written on parenting, but no book is better or greater than the Word of God. It's amazing how often we'll look for self-help books to fix this or that, or teach us this or that, but very seldom will we ever consider the bible as a first option. Have you ever wondered why its normally not even an option? More often than not, we'll seek advice from family or friends, social media, or the latest parenting book or magazine. We have no problem consulting a medical professional when our child is sick or a teacher regarding their education. Given this respect for experts, why is seeking God regarding the upbringing, direction, and spiritual growth of children a last resort or not considered at all?

Children will mimic the character and values of their parents. If you are a parent raising your child in a home filled with love where you demonstrate godly character and enforce the importance of God's Word, it will reflect in your children. Contrary to that, parents who are not present and lacking self-control in their behavior will produce those same characteristics in their children. Parents must also be mindful that children pay more attention to what their mother and father do as oppose to what they say. When your actions and speech don't match, it confuses your child(ren) and does not produce righteousness in them.

Parents must also discipline their children. Contrary to popular belief, discipline is not a bad word. It means: "control gained by enforcing obedience or order; orderly or prescribed conduct or pattern of behavior; training that corrects, molds, or perfects the mental faculties or moral character" (Merriam Webster). The key to discipline is having a healthy balance between non-punitive and punitive punishment that increases in severity to include corrective communication and discipline.

Non-Punitive Discipline

This is not punishing a child for inappropriate behavior, but rather relying on communication. With the understanding that if the child's basic physical and emotional needs are met, he will be able to act accordingly or be able to correct and compose himself with minimal input or assistance from the parent. Non-punitive disciplining involves establishing clear boundaries, taking your child out of the situation, and making a big deal out of good behavior. An example of this type of discipline can be as simple as having your child go to his or her room because they are acting out or not behaving.

Punitive Discipline

This is a rebuke or reprimand as a form of communication to correct behavior (chastisement). It also includes punishment by inflicting pain, penalty and/or loss, to include spanking. Appropriate examples of punitive punishment are grounding, isolation (time out), withdrawing or withholding, logical consequences, and spanking.

Naturally, there are some rules for parental punishment in order to keep it constructive and from becoming abusive. The anger of man does not produce the righteousness of Christ. (James 1:20)

1. Discipline should never be given in anger.

Parents should be calm and measured when disciplining a child.

2. Discipline should be equal to the behavior.

Parents must discern the difference between childishness and foolishness. Foolishness should be punished, and childishness should be corrected.

3. Discipline should be consistent.

Discipline must be consistent. An unacceptable action needs to be met with consistent punitive and non-punitive action each time. In addition, the giving of discipline should also be consistent between parents.

4. Discipline should create closeness not distance.

When a child is being disobedient to his or her parent, distance is created in the relationship. However, when the parent disciplines his or her child, it shouldn't create a greater distance; it should restore closeness.

As parents we need to establish a solid foundation in Christ for our children. We should model godly character before them, exposing them to the Word of God, teaching them to memorize scripture, showing them how to pray, and reminding them that God is love. In doing these things we help our children establish a personal relationship with God.

Establishing a solid foundation within our children also means helping to develop their character. We do this by showing and teaching them respect for themselves and others, helping them form clear morals and values, teaching good manners, imparting how to take ownership of one's actions, and modeling the ability to compromise. These actions and manners of behaving will equip them for what they will need to succeed in this world.

Just recently we were informed by our daughter how our grandchild had been acting up at his daycare. We encouraged our daughter to establish a routine of prayer with him each morning prior to going to school as well as implementing consequences for his misbehavior, including limited television and playtime. She further informed us that whenever he wasn't allowed to do or have something he wanted at school, he acted out by folding his arms, pouting, and or even attempting to hit and kick his teachers. Almost daily, they were receiving phone calls and reports about his misbehavior.

My wife and I continued to pray and ask the Lord for wisdom and direction concerning this situation. My wife was led to a book we already had by Frank and Ida Mae Hammond called *A Manual for Children's Deliverance*. In chapter 4, Deliverance Methods, they teach about the authority we have as believers to pray and lay hands on children just as Jesus did. "Then some children were brought to Him so that he might lay his hands on them and pray." (Matt. 19:13a)

With this new revelation and knowledge, my wife began to pray more boldly and fervently for our grandson whenever he began to act out while in our care. She recalled an incident where he was beginning to get upset because she told him no, so she placed his face in her hands and had him look directly at her. She began to pray a prayer of deliverance binding the strongman that was manifesting in his behavior by applying the shed blood of Jesus Christ. She said immediately he began to calm himself down and listen. When she called and told me what had happened, I almost couldn't believe it happened that quick. Thank you, Jesus, for watching over your word to perform it. Now whenever my grandson sees the Bible, he calls it the Jesus Book that calms him down.

My daughter posted a conversation on social media she had with her son on the way home from daycare. "How was school today?" He answered, "Mommy, this boy in my class was on red today because he was hitting. I was on green today, so I got my treat. I told him to ask Jesus to calm his body down when he got angry." What an amazing testimony from the mouth of a child! Did I mention my grandson is only 3 years old?

It's never too early to teach your children or any other children the Word of God because, just as they can retain songs and sounds, they enjoy, they can retain the word of God. "Train up a child in the way he should go: and when he is old, he will not depart from it." (Prov. 22:6)

10.

Graduation

There is no standard formula for finding a spouse. However, the challenges and issues marriages face are not unique to any one marriage. Just as in the military, all marriages must go through bootcamp (basic training), regardless of your background, economic or social status, etc. In order to be a member of the armed forces, this training step cannot be bypassed. Whether recruits make it through the first time or have to repeat a week or more is dependent upon the individual. In marriage, all couples will have to deal with at minimum the issues of commitment, communication, conflict and finances. How these issues are dealt with are dependent upon the couple.

The process to complete bootcamp is planned in detail for each week. Recruits know what is expected and what is required. Also, in marriage, the blueprint is laid out in detail in the Word of God. The Bible informs us what is expected and what is required. The principles and strategies set by God are foundational standards for all marriages to follow.

Help is available, but are you both willing to set pride or whatever is hindering you aside to repair and strengthen your marriage? This is a question we believe everyone must answer because no marriage is exempt from the issues of life. "I have told you these things, so that in me you may have peace. In this world you will have trouble. But take heart! I have overcome the world." (John 16:33) Just as basic training is designed to prepare us for our military careers, we sincerely believe the Word of God can help prepare us all for marriage.

With that in mind, we were inspired to write this book. If through our experiences we can help one marriage, then our labor was not in vain. God created man and woman to be as one in marriage, and what He has joined together, let no one split apart (Mark 10:8-9).